# THE SHELL POSTER BOOK

First published in Great Britain in 1998 by
PROFILE BOOKS LTD
62 QUEEN ANNE STREET
LONDON W1M 9LA

Copyright © Shell U.K. Limited 1998

Printed in Italy by Artegrafica S.p.A

A CIP catalogue record for this book is available from the British Library.

ISBN 1 86197 061 7

# FOREWORD

## BY LORD MONTAGU OF BEAULIEU

I was delighted when Shell agreed in 1992 to move their famous art collection from a storeroom in Shell-Mex House on the Strand to the National Motor Museum at Beaulieu. Beaulieu was considered to be the natural venue for the art collection which has such close ties with the history of motoring. Here, the posters and paintings are located close to the Museum's historical motoring archive and the extensive collection of vehicles.

At Beaulieu the collection has been organised and catalogued on a picture database. Parts of the collection regularly go out on exhibition to other museums and galleries and there is a permanent display at the Motor Museum gallery.

The most celebrated part of the Shell Art Collection are the lorry bills produced in the 1920s and 1930s. These were commissioned by Jack Beddington, the advertising manager at Shell, who had a keen eye for young talent and was adept at coming up with good ideas. His ability to spot young artists and allow them to produce original and innovative advertisements made the campaigns of his era such a success. Many of the best known artists of this period worked on posters for Shell, including Graham Sutherland, Paul Nash, Ben Nicholson, Hans Feibusch, Vanessa Bell and the graphic designer Edward McKnight Kauffer – many, as in the case of Graham Sutherland, producing their first professional work for Shell.

The posters from this period have a stunning visual impact. There are examples of many different styles and influences, from the memorable vorticist image of 'Mousehole, Cornwall' by A. Stuart-Hill to Paul Nash's semi-abstract 'Footballers Prefer Shell'.

The posters were originally displayed on boards on the side of delivery lorries and series such as 'Visit Britain's Landmarks' and 'These People Prefer Shell', in a subtle way, encouraged people to get out and enjoy the countryside in their cars.

Although the Second World War ended this period of advertising glory and changes in the design of lorries in the 1950s meant that posters were no longer displayed in the same way, Shell continued with their patronage of the arts, producing County Guides and nature pictures for educational and advertising purposes. With the encouragement of Shell, Jack Beddington joined the well known London advertising agency, Colman Prentis and Varley, who handled the Shell advertising account. I got to know Jack Beddington well in the 1950s, as he recommended me for my first job at Colman Prentis and Varley when I left Oxford.

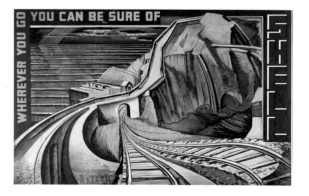

This unique collection has found a fitting place at the National Motor Museum, where it complements the vehicles and artefacts from the period when the artwork was produced. The display generates interest from other galleries, museums and the public, enabling the posters to continue to play an important role in the cultural life of Britain today.

# INTRODUCTION

## BY JOHN HEWITT

The posters in this book are lorry bills produced by Shell between 1920 and 1953. These bills were an unusual form of mobile outdoor advertising. They were framed posters of a standard size, 30″ x 40″, attached to the sides and back of Shell lorries delivering cans of petrol and oil to customers all over the country. The lorry bills were not the only outdoor advertising used by Shell in this period. In the 1920s they had used placards and enamelled signs outside garages and along country roads until the company removed them in response to pressure from groups like the Council for the Protection of Rural England (CPRE). Throughout the inter-war period the company also made use of fixed hoardings, particularly in the late 1930s when large posters were attached to solus sites. However, by far the most common and typical form of advertising was the lorry bills. It was this advertising campaign that established the company as outstanding advertisers of taste and discernment during the 1930s.

It was different in the 1920s when Shell's witty and sophisticated press advertising won the plaudits. In many ways the lorry bills of this decade were more functional in their message. In common with most outdoor advertising in the 1920s Shell's lorry bills display the commodity, identify the user and define the use to which it could be

put. This is clearly evident in the first seven bills illustrated in this collection, all of which show either cans of oil or motor cars. As a strategy it was little different from that adopted by most manufacturers of this period.

The lorry bills also identified Shell's innovations in the new pumps for delivering oil (11, 12, 14). This reinforced the modern approach of the company and helped to draw attention to the pumps which motorists could then immediately recognise when they drew up on a garage forecourt. It is easy to forget that during the inter-war period garages sold more than one brand of petrol and there was a wide variety of pumps competing for the motorist's attention.

Much of Shell's advertising in the 1920s was 'reason-to-buy' advertising, stressing the virtues of the products. This could be done by a series of assertions (18, 19, 26) or more obliquely by underlining the modernity of the product (17, 20, 23). More typical of contemporary advertising was the use of a clever and memorable slogan that would be reinforced by a powerful image. This was seen to greatest effect in campaign slogans like 'Quick Starting Pair' (15, 16, 21, 25, 30, 31, 34, 39) 'Pull' (33) and the witty 'That's Shell That Was' (57). All of which also testify to the reliability and power of the products.

As with other advertising in this period, Shell developed campaigns in which press and poster advertising was carefully coordinated. The campaign themes were reinforced and elaborated in newspapers and journals in the 1920s. In fact it is striking how mainstream Shell advertising was in the 1920s. This may account for the company's tendency to use commercial rather than fine artists to produce their advertising designs.

Of course there were exceptions. The cartoonist H.M. Bateman and the fine artist D.C. Fouqueray, are both more traditional and 'establishment' illustrators. In fact, their posters (5, 7, 8) allude to a motoring public drawn from the upper middle classes and upper classes who typified the private motorists of the 1920s. This was a social class attuned to the sophistication and wit of much of Shell's press advertising at the time. It was also a class that celebrated the exciting possibilities afforded by the relatively new pastime of motoring.

During the 1930s the emphasis in the lorry bills began to change. There was progressively less focus on 'reason-to-buy' advertising and a more indirect appeal to the consumer's taste. The company was marketed rather than its oil and petrol. References to these products became marginalised and finally disappeared in those increasingly typical posters that celebrated Britain's natural and historical delights with slogans like 'See Britain First on Shell' (35,36,37,38), 'Everywhere You Can Be Sure of Shell' (41-4, 46-51, 53-5, 59, 60, 61, 74, 100, 103, 104),

THESE MEN USE SHELL

YOU CAN BE SURE OF SHELL

FARMERS   JOHN ARMSTRONG

'To Visit Britain's Landmarks You Can Be Sure of Shell' (71-3, 75, 76, 78, 81-6) and in those campaigns asserting that certain professions and trades 'Prefer Shell' (32, 52, 56, 62-5, 67, 68, 70, 77) or that 'These Men Use Shell' (87-95). It was never made clear why they preferred to use it. It was enough that they did. Company and user underlined the taste and judgement of each other in a process of mutual reinforcement.

In the 1930s many of Shell's posters were of fine landmarks, historical sights and inspiring landscapes, all firmly located in the countryside. It was an idealised view of a rural order much sought after by the middle-classes, particularly those from the towns. By celebrating and making accessible such rural delights, Shell won the plaudits of powerful pressure groups who sought to protect the countryside from urban expansion and the destruction of rural amenities by advertising hoardings. An indication of how closely Shell worked with such pressure groups was demonstrated in their choice of Clough William-Ellis, a major figure in the CPRE, to open their first exhibition of Shell posters at the New Burlington Galleries in June 1931.

In effect, Shell was encouraging motorists to use Shell petrol and oil to visit all these rural delights. But such visits were only possible because of the recent accessibility of the countryside in this new motoring age. The paradoxes of Shell's policy were kept at bay by removing from many of their lorry bills the symbols of modernity like the car, the road, telegraph poles, garages and restaurants. Though many of these views were presented in a modern art style none of them celebrated the contemporary world. In much of the advertising during the 1930s, reference to the qualities of Shell's petrol and oil, its quick starting qualities and its power, were more obliquely reinforced (compare 26 and 34). The one exception to this development was the use of posters to advise motorists to change from winter to summer oil and vice-versa, a necessity in the days before multigrade, though even here the references were far from blatant (58, 66, 69).

Shell exhibited its advertising at two more exhibitions in the 1930s, again at the New Burlington Galleries in 1934 and at Shell-Mex House in 1938. Both exhibitions were opened by Sir Kenneth Clark, the Director of the National Gallery at the time. In this way, Shell's name became linked to the prestige and euphoric values of fine art. A whole array of fine artists were used in the 1930s and the company was seen as a patron of the arts. Their advertising, along with that of the London Underground, Imperial Airways and the main railway companies, was recognised as the very best of the period. Most of the leading modernist

artists in England between the wars, from Vanessa Bell (36), Duncan Grant (50), John Armstrong (48, 56, 94, 103), Tristram Hillier (65, 77) to Paul Nash (51, 68, 85), Graham Sutherland (44, 47, 86) and Ben Nicholson (88) all designed for Shell. It is a dazzling list of talent. Perhaps providing designs for petrol company advertising fitted with their sense of modernity: art in and for the modern spirit. But this was also art for a purpose. Rarely did the artists' designs go to the extremes of their easel work. For instance, only in the bottom right-hand corner of Ben Nicholson's poster design (88) is there any hint of the abstract art he was working on in 1938. The designs were invariably figurative and defined a coherent three-dimensional space. One rarely needed to puzzle over the beauty spot or profession being referred to.

Shell did not only commission modern painters. Traditional artists like J.D.M. Harvey, Algernon Newton, Dacres Adams (28), Rex Whistler (55) and Lord Berners (75) were also employed in the 1930s. It was as if Shell wanted all English art to be displayed on its lorry bills and not merely the modernist variation. The company benefited from its association with 'art' not the avant-garde. The way in which the

company commissioned artists to produce the design but kept the advertising slogans from encroaching on the image, the way the posters were framed, exhibited and reviewed throughout the 1930s, all contributed to their status as art. Shell was praised as a patron of discernment and an advertiser of responsibility. It brought art out of the academy and onto the roads so that everyone could benefit from this people's picture gallery. Of course, this also deflected growing criticism of other outdoor publicity which was seen as tasteless and vulgar.

In the 1930s Shell had a brilliant and creative advertising manager, Jack Beddington, who became responsible for commissioning the designers and artists who made the advertising of the 1930s so distinctive. (There is a portrait of him in a poster by John Armstrong (94).) Beddington took sole responsibility for the lorry bills, leaving press advertising to the Regent Advertising Service, an agency owned by the company. This meant that there was less evidence of coordinated press and poster advertising from the 1930s onwards.

Two other factors explain the change of policy. Firstly, 1930s petrol companies were no longer in competition with each other over price. In fact, Shell-Mex UK also took responsibility for the marketing of BP's petrol. Nor were there many technical differences between the different petrols until the late 1930s. Consequently, competition was not at the level of price and quality but of brand image. Thus Shell increasingly concentrated on corporate rather than product advertising. Secondly, Shell was selling its petrol to a different consumer in the

1930s. During the 1920s Shell appealed to a small wealthy group who owned cars. This is evident in the individuals represented in the stylish art deco poster of René Vincent (14) and the clubland humour of H.M. Bateman (5). Where the countryside was shown as in D.C. Fouqueray's 'Sma' Glen, Crieff' (8) it appeared as a backcloth against which motorists strolled or picnicked. This was their world and if they didn't own it they were at ease in it. By contrast, the views on offer in Shell's posters of the 1930s were of a different order. They represented places visited by a suburban middle-class benefiting from the massive expansion of motoring. They were on the outside looking in and the very structure of the posters reinforced that fact.

Not all the Shell posters of the 1930s were engaged with art and nature. There were still references to the technical virtues of the petrol and this continued after the Second World War as the posters of the early 1950s show (98, 99, 101, 102, 105, 106).

The outstanding and distinctive period in Shell's poster advertising came to an end in 1953 when the lorry gave way to the petrol tanker. It also coincided with the increased use of photography in advertising and the decline of graphic posters. Fortunately, the posters from this heyday have all been preserved and are recognised as fine pieces of art in their own right. Today they can be appreciated by everyone reading this book or visiting the National Motor Museum at Beaulieu.

JOHN HEWITT                    Manchester Metropolitan University

1  1920

3  1921

5 H M Bateman, 1924

# SHELL

distributes more petrol
refined from crude oils

## PRODUCED WITHIN THE BRITISH EMPIRE

than all the other petrol
distributing Companies
in Great Britain combined.

7  D C Fouqueray, 1925

SMA' GLEN, CRIEFF

SEE BRITAIN FIRST -

SEE IRELAND FIRST -

ON SHELL

GLENDALOUGH

9  Barker, 1925

11  1925

SEE IRELAND FIRST -

ON SHELL

GIANTS' CAUSEWAY
ULSTER

13  Barker, 1925

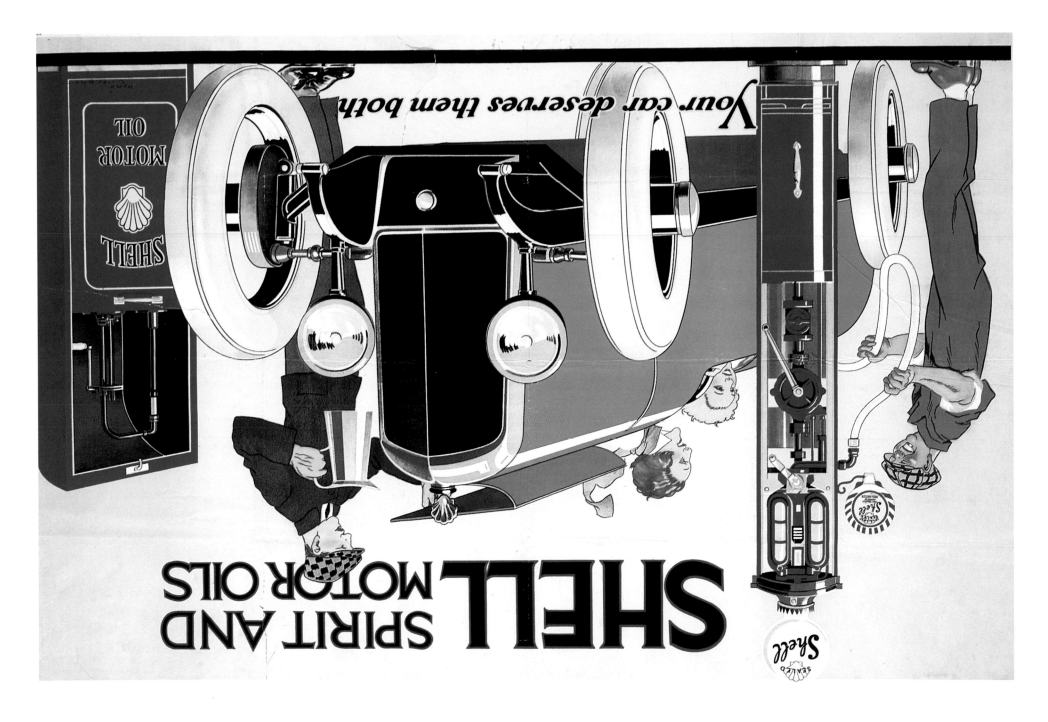

15 Jean D'Ylen, 1926

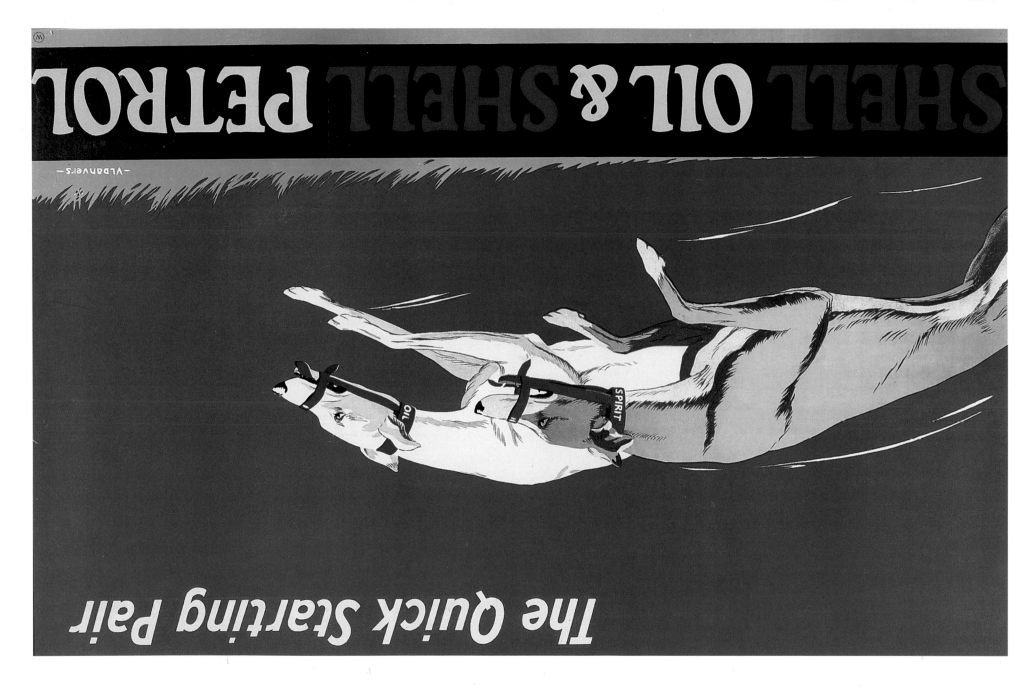

17 Tom Purvis, 1928

19  1928

But for MODERN lubrication—
SHELL OIL . . . .

21 Shell Studio, 1928

23  Tom Purvis, 1928

25  C Paine, 1928

27  F C Harrison, 1928

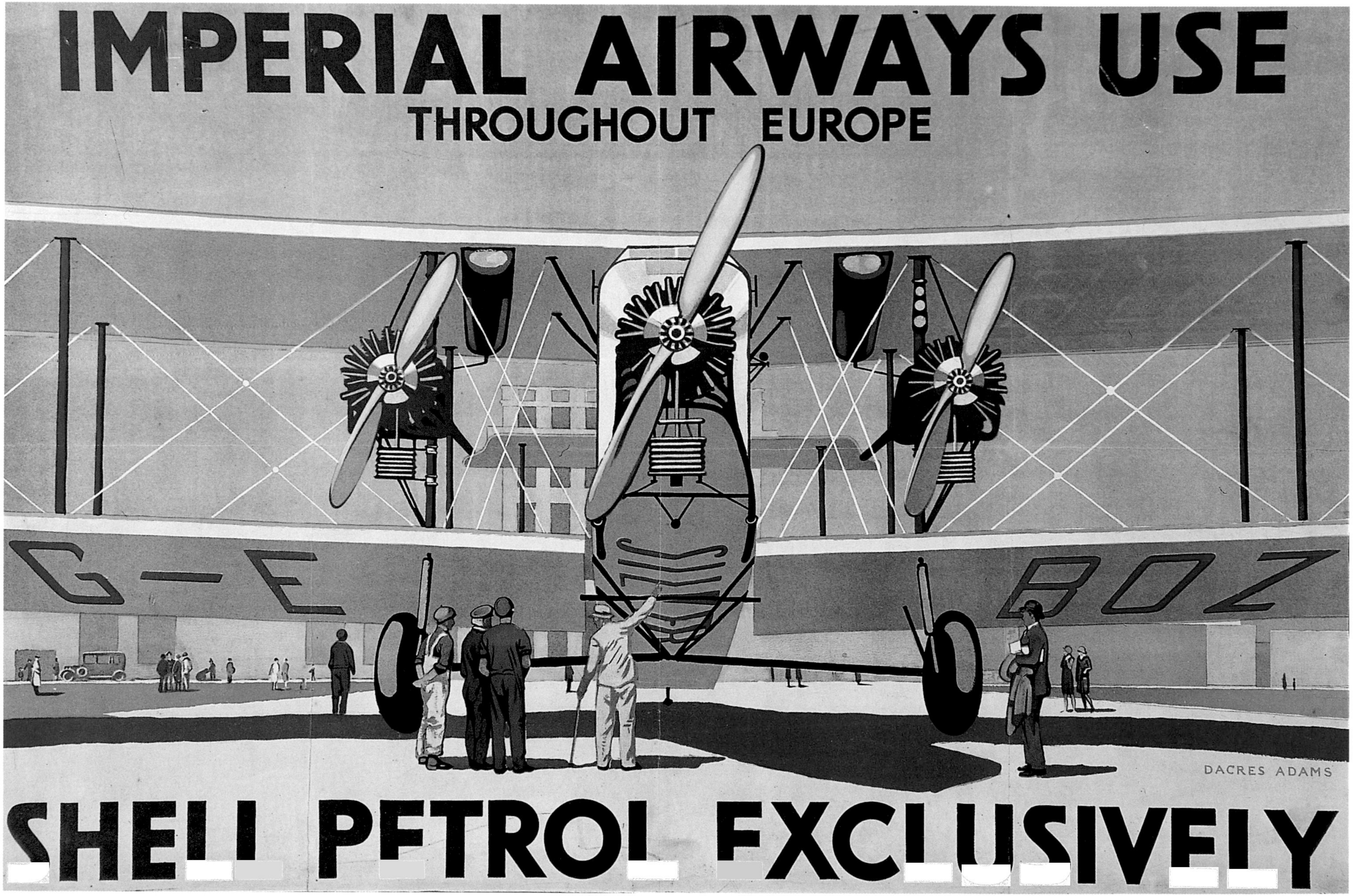


28 Dacres Adams, 1929

29 Yunge, 1930

31  James Holland, 1930

33  Tom Purvis, 1930

SHELL OIL AND PETROL THE QUICK STARTING PAIR

THE GIANT CERNE ABBAS

SEE BRITAIN FIRST ON SHELL

35  F Dobson, 1931

ALFRISTON

# SEE BRITAIN FIRST ON SHELL

36  Vanessa Bell, 1931

37  Edward McKnight Kauffer, 1931

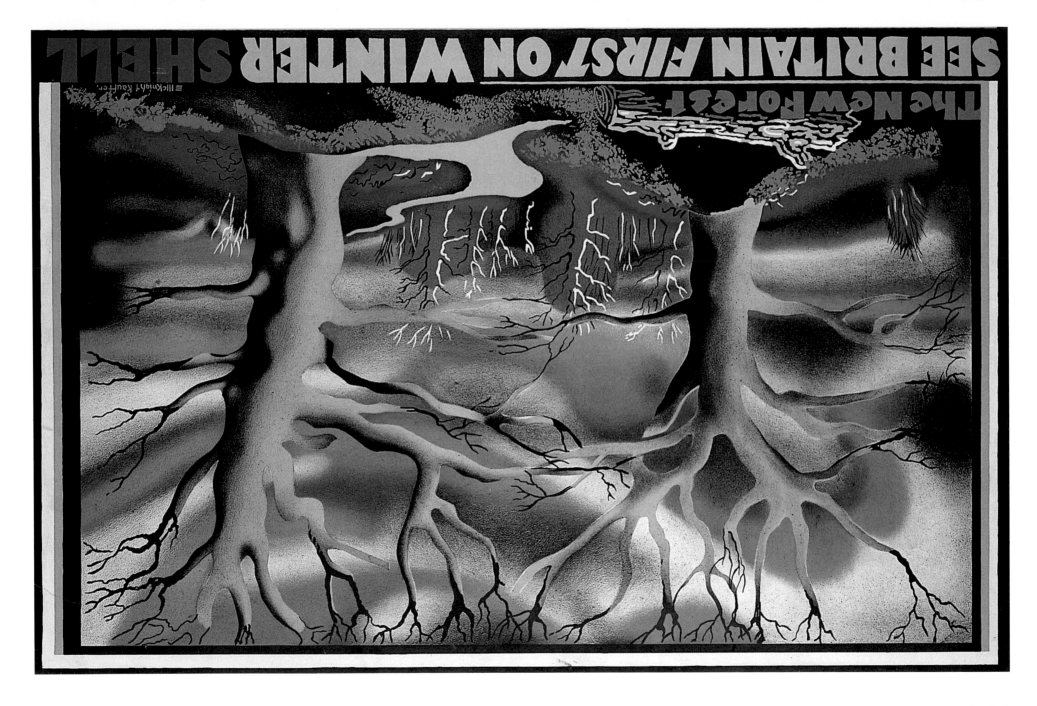

SEE BRITAIN FIRST ON WINTER SHELL

The New Forest

E McKnight Kauffer.

39  Rowe, 1931

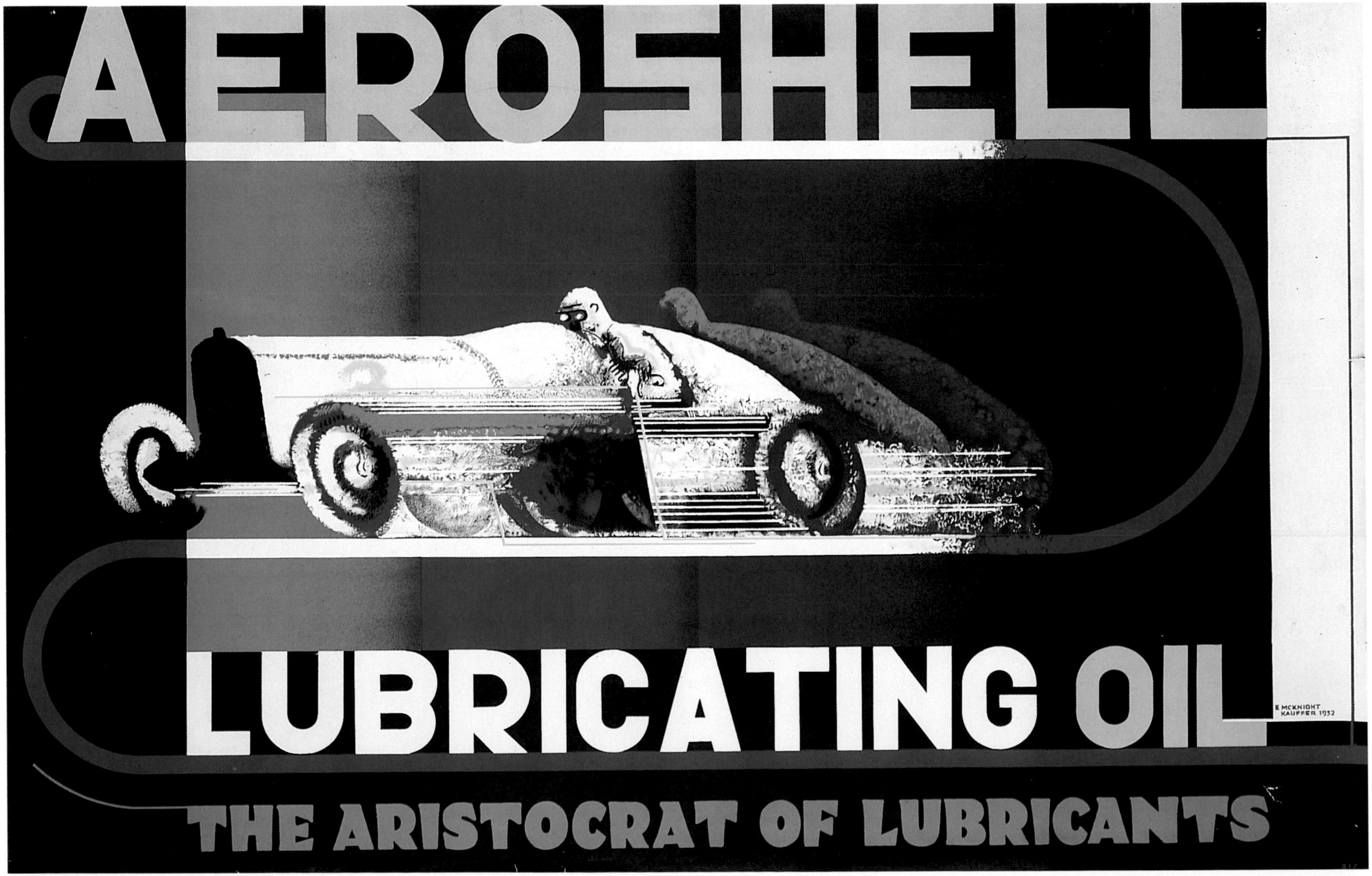


40 Edward McKnight Kauffer 1932

41 Edward McKnight Kauffer, 1932

# Everywhere you go—

CASTLE HOWARD Co.WICKLOW

BY G. BISSILL

# YOU CAN BE SURE OF SHELL

No.314

# EVERYWHERE YOU GO

MARWOOD, NORTH DEVON.

By ERIC GEORGE.

# YOU CAN BE SURE OF SHELL

43  Eric George, 1932

YOU CAN BE SURE OF SHELL

NR LEEDS, KENT.

BY GRAHAM SUTHERLAND

EVERYWHERE YOU GO

FOR RELIABILITY—

ATALANTA CLASS AIR LINER    BARNETT FREEDMAN

SHELL LUBRICATING OIL

45  Barnett Freedman, 1932

# EVERYWHERE YOU GO

SWALEDALE, YORKSHIRE

BARNETT FREEDMAN.

# YOU CAN BE SURE OF SHELL

THE GREAT GLOBE. SWANAGE.

BY GRAHAM SUTHERLAND

47  Graham Sutherland, 1932

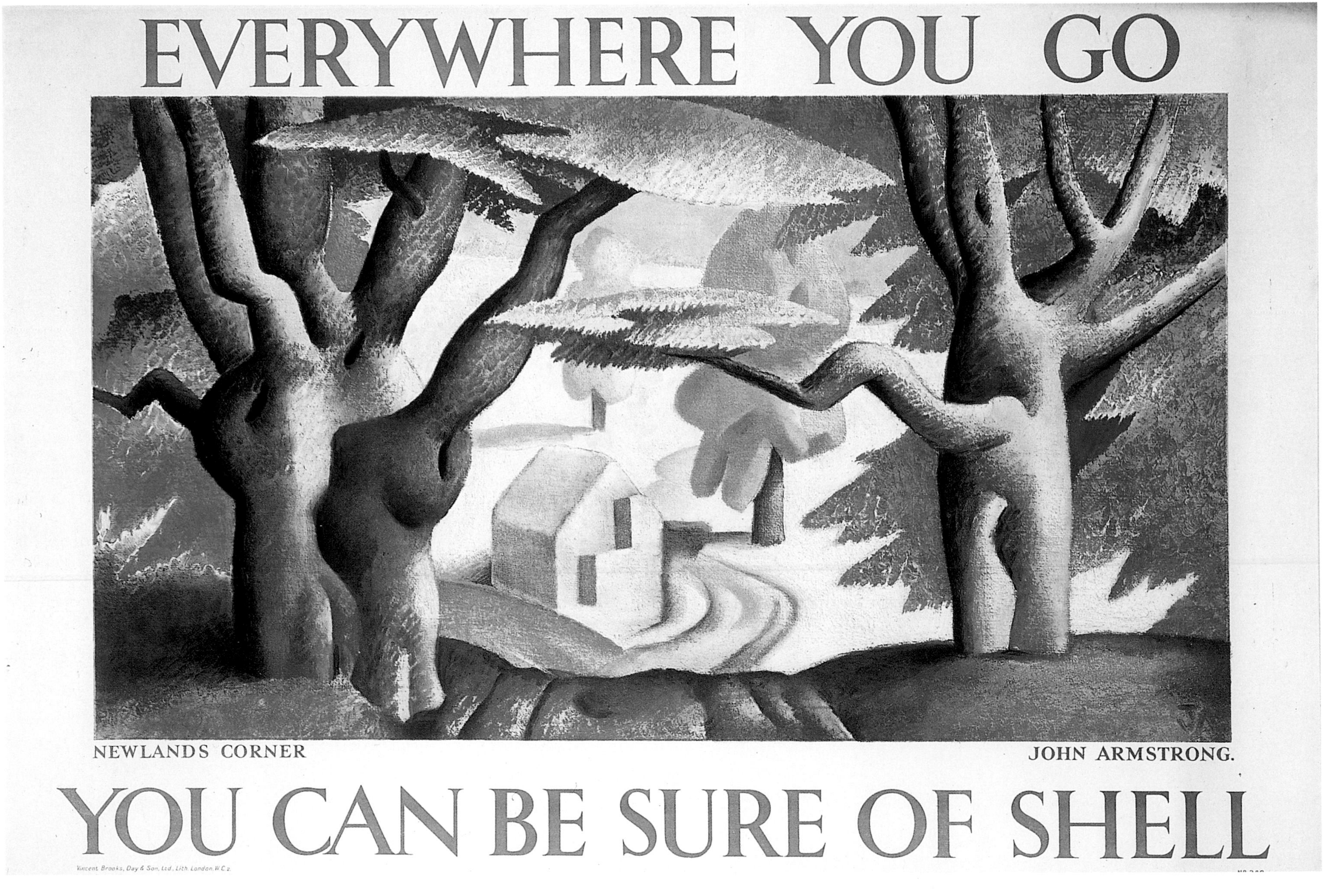


48 John Armstrong 1932

49  A Stuart-Hill, 1932

YOU CAN BE SURE OF SHELL

EVERYWHERE YOU GO

ST. IVES HUNTINGDON BY DUNCAN GRANT

EVERYWHERE YOU GO

THE RYE MARSHES

PAUL NASH

YOU CAN BE SURE OF SHELL

51  Paul Nash, 1932

# ARCHITECTS PREFER SHELL

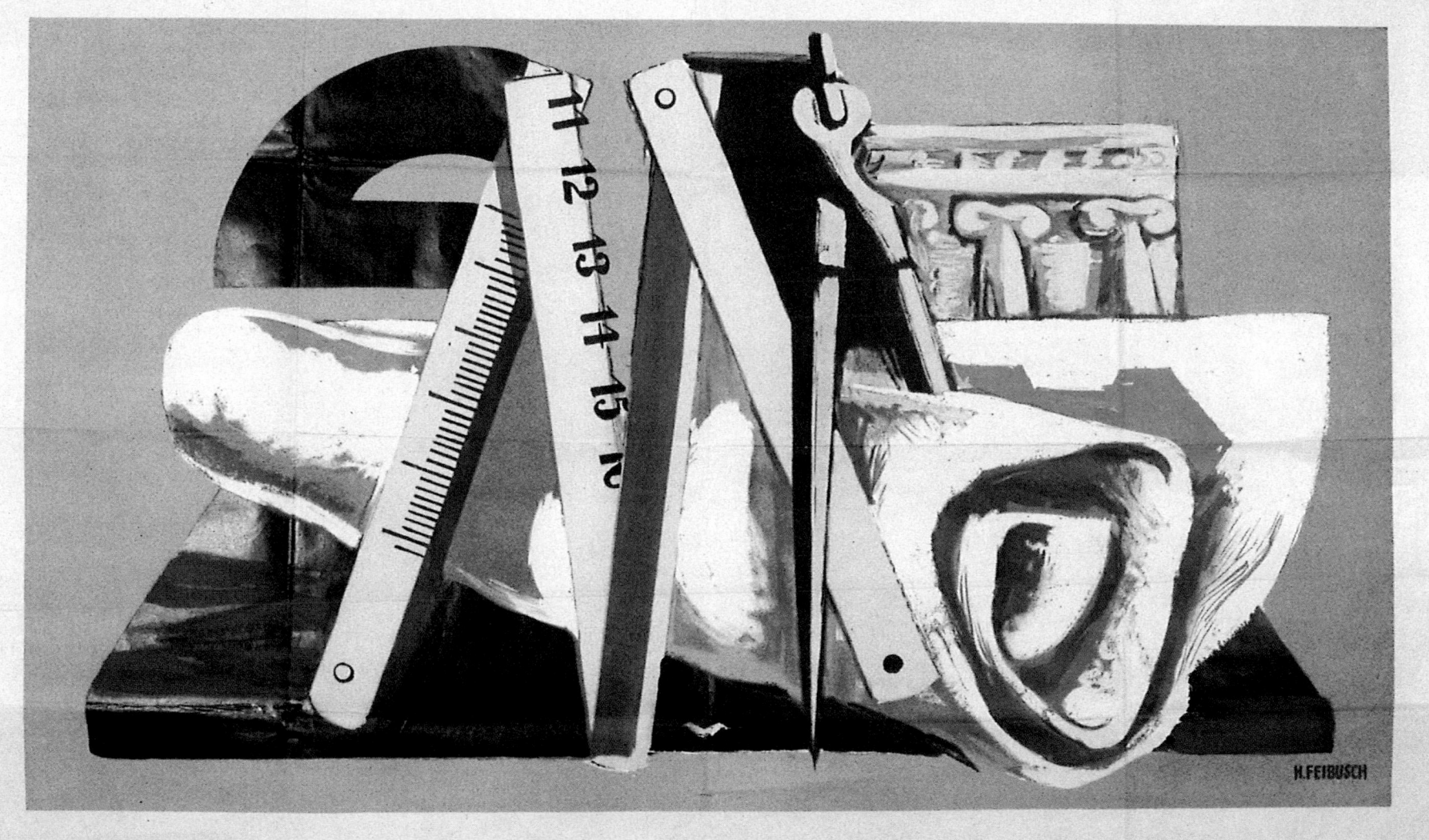

# YOU CAN BE SURE OF SHELL

52  Hans Feibusch. 1933

# EVERYWHERE YOU GO

WESTWYCOMBE.

C. MANN.

# YOU CAN BE SURE OF SHELL

53  Cathleen Mann, 1933

No 373.

Vincent Brooks Day & Son Ltd. Lith. London W.C.2

# YOU CAN BE SURE OF SHELL

GENERAL WADES BRIDGE, ABERFELDY.

EDWIN CALLIGAN.

Edwin Calligan

# EVERYWHERE YOU GO

# EVERYWHERE YOU GO

THE VALE OF AYLESBURY

REX WHISTLER

# YOU CAN BE SURE OF SHELL

55  Rex Whistler, 1933

57  John Reynolds, 1933

# EVERYWHERE YOU GO

POLPERRO CORNWALL.

By M.A.MILES.

# YOU CAN BE SURE OF SHELL

59 Maurice A Miles, 1933

YOU CAN BE SURE OF SHELL

GORDALE SCAR - THE CRAVEN FAULT, YORKS.          EDGAR AINSWORTH

EVERYWHERE YOU GO

EVERYWHERE YOU GO

LOWER SLAUGHTER.

ROSEMARY & CLIFFORD ELLIS 1934.

ROSEMARY & CLIFFORD ELLIS.

YOU CAN BE SURE OF SHELL

61  Rosemary & Clifford Ellis, 1934

63  Rosemary and Clifford Ellis, 1934

65  Tristram Hillier, 1934

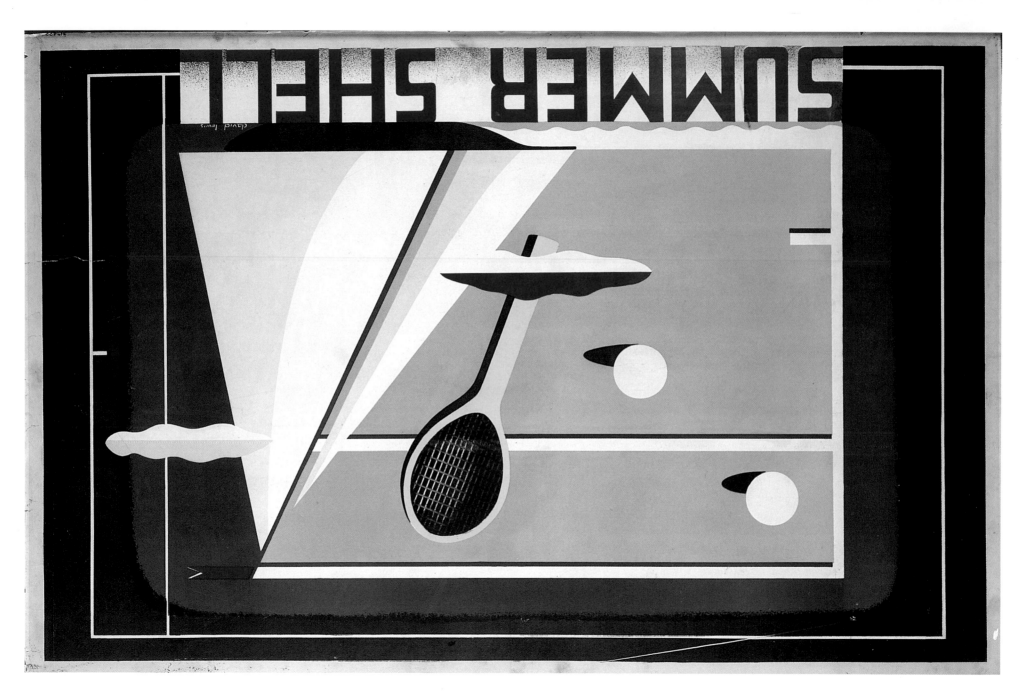

SUMMER SHELL

david lewis

67 J S Anderson, 1935

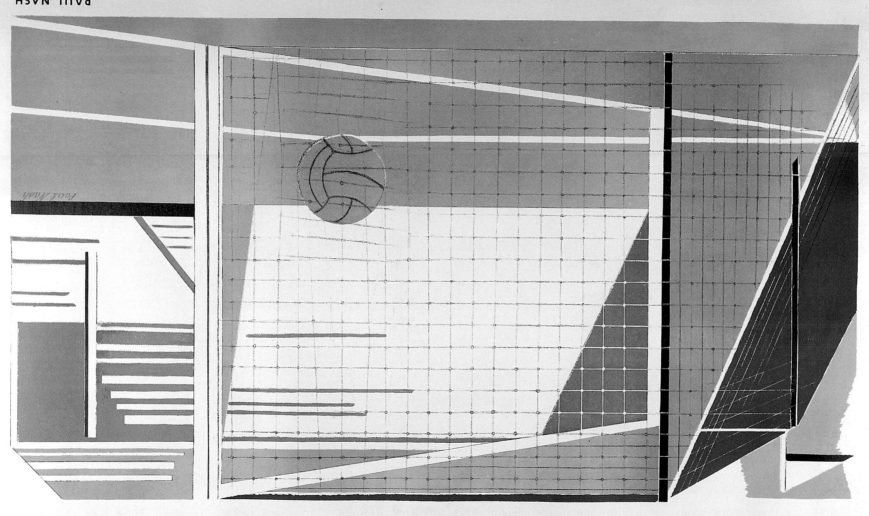

FOOTBALLERS PREFER SHELL

PAUL NASH

YOU CAN BE SURE OF SHELL

69  Jack Miller, 1936

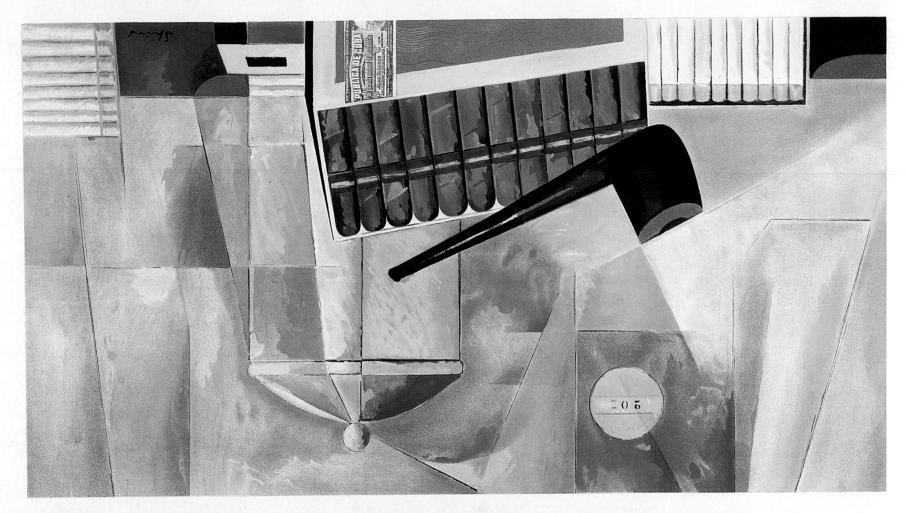

71 Edward McKnight Kauffer, 1936

TO VISIT BRITAIN'S LANDMARKS

RALPH ALLEN'S SHAM CASTLE NEAR BATH                    RICHARD GUYATT

YOU CAN BE SURE OF SHELL

73  Richard Guyatt, 1936

# EVERYWHERE YOU GO

DEVIL'S ELBOW, BRAEMAR                                        ROBERT MILLER

# YOU CAN BE SURE OF SHELL

74  Robert Miller 1936

TO VISIT BRITAIN'S LANDMARKS

FARINGDON FOLLY

LORD BERNERS

YOU CAN BE SURE OF SHELL

75. Lord Berners, 1936

# TO VISIT BRITAIN'S LANDMARKS

JOHN KNOX MONUMENT, GLASGOW.

PAMELA DREW

# YOU CAN BE SURE OF SHELL

# TOURISTS PREFER SHELL

# YOU CAN BE SURE OF SHELL

77 Tristram Hillier, 1936

YOU CAN BE SURE OF SHELL

"ROMAN" TOWER, TUTBURY, STAFFS.

L. H. ROSOMAN

TO VISIT BRITAIN'S LANDMARKS

79  Tom Gentleman, 1936

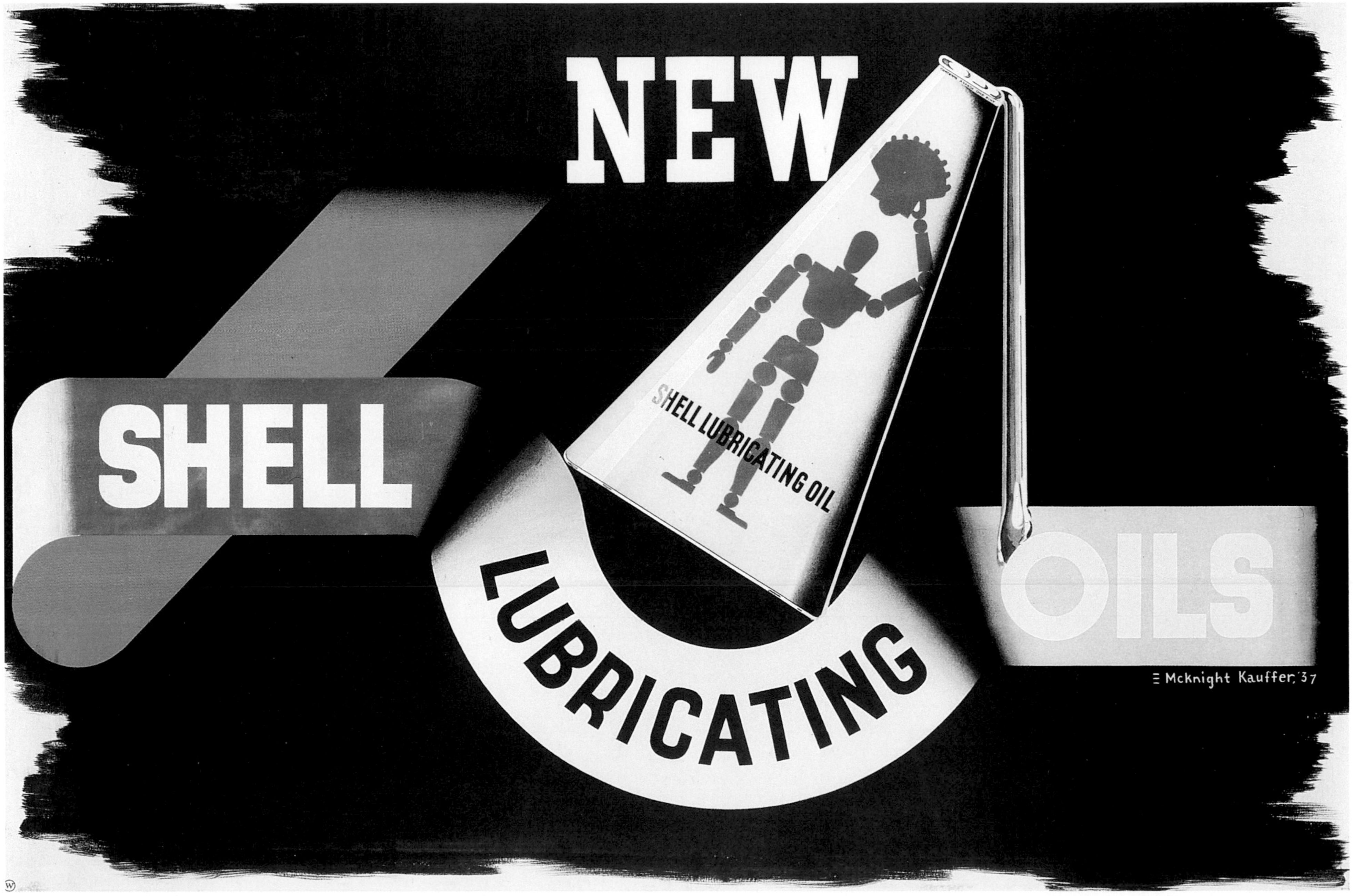


80 Edward McKnight Kauffer 1937

TO VISIT BRITAIN'S LANDMARKS

A STRANGE CHURCH, AYOT St. LAWRENCE, HERTS.

T. GENTLEMAN

YOU CAN BE SURE OF SHELL

81  Tom Gentleman, 1937

TEMPLE BAR             EDWARD SCROGGIE

# TO VISIT BRITAIN'S LANDMARKS

FOLLY HOUSES, DARLEY ABBEY

ROWLAND SUDDABY

# YOU CAN BE SURE OF SHELL

83 Rowland Suddaby, 1937

YOU CAN BE SURE OF SHELL

CHANTER'S FOLLY AND DRY DOCK, APPLEDORE.

CLIFFORD AND ROSEMARY ELLIS

TO VISIT BRITAIN'S LANDMARKS

TO VISIT BRITAIN'S LANDMARKS

KIMMERIDGE FOLLY, DORSET

PAUL NASH

YOU CAN BE SURE OF SHELL

85 Paul Nash, 1937

TO VISIT BRITAIN'S LANDMARKS

BRIMHAM ROCK, YORKSHIRE

GRAHAM SUTHERLAND

YOU CAN BE SURE OF SHELL

# THESE MEN USE SHELL

EDWARD ARDIZZONE

# YOU CAN BE SURE OF SHELL

87  Edward Ardizzone, 1938

# THESE MEN USE SHELL

SIGHTSEERS

C. MOZLEY

# YOU CAN BE SURE OF SHELL

89  Charles Mozley, 1938

# FILM STARS USE SHELL

C. MANN

# YOU CAN BE SURE OF SHELL

90. Cathleen Mann, 1938

# THESE MEN USE SHELL

JOURNALISTS

ZERO

# YOU CAN BE SURE OF SHELL

91  Hans Schleger (ZERO), 1938

93  Charles Mozley, 1939

95  Richard Guyatt, 1939

97 Abram Games, 1939

**NEW LIFE TO THE LAND**

 **SHELL TRACTOR OILS**

99  Joseph Webb, 1951

# EVERYWHERE YOU GO

Culzean Castle and Ailsa Craig

Robin Darwin

# YOU CAN BE SURE OF SHELL

100 R Darwin 1952

101  George Chapman, 1952

and feel the difference

fill up with SHELL

# EVERYWHERE YOU GO

Near Lamorna

John Armstrong

# YOU CAN BE SURE OF SHELL

103 John Armstrong, 1952

# EVERYWHERE YOU GO

Arlington Row, Bibury

Mary Kessell

# YOU CAN BE SURE OF SHELL

105  George Ayers, 1952

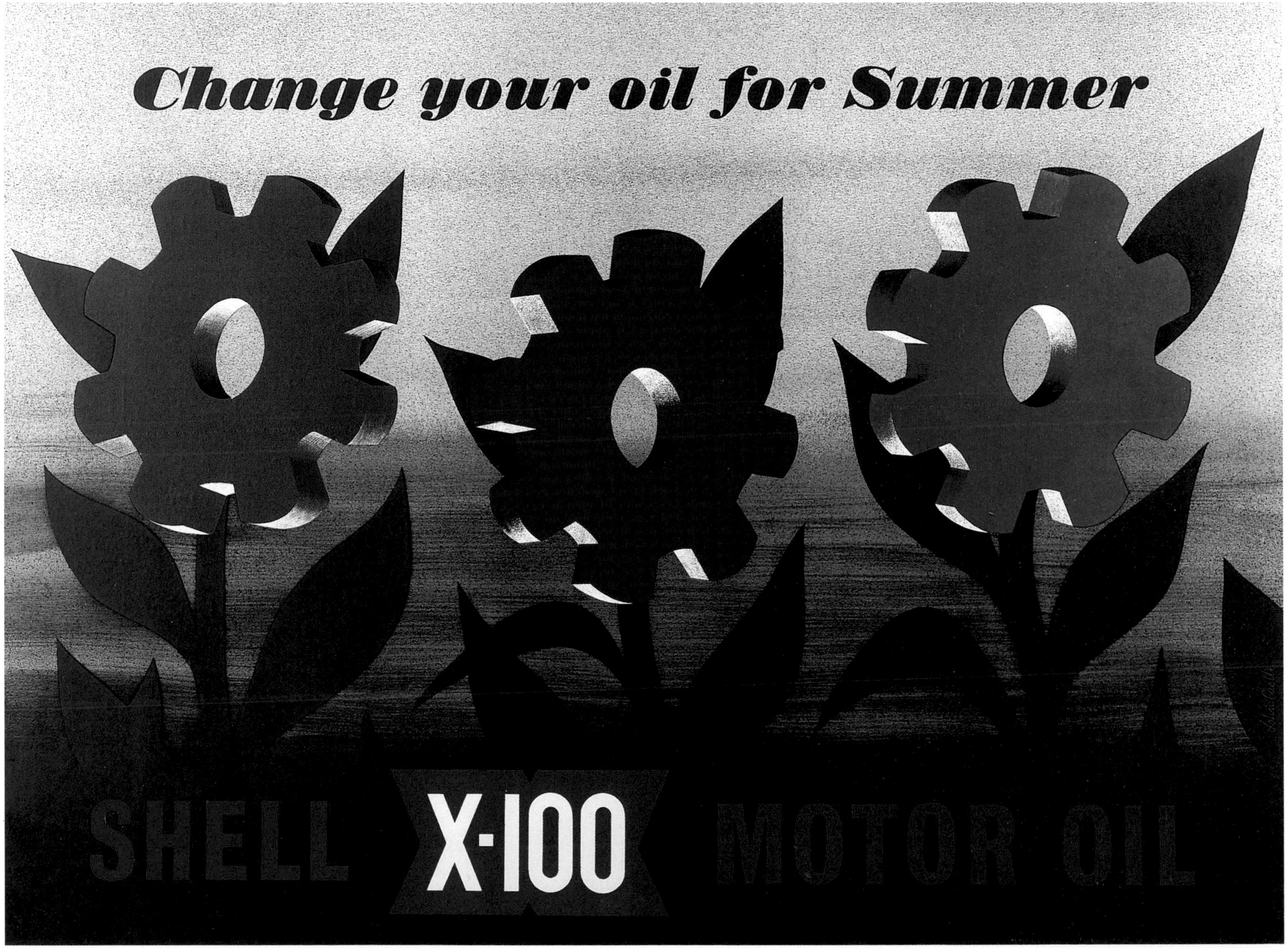


106 John Castle 1958

107 *Clergymen Prefer Shell* by John Piper, commissioned by Shell in 1930 but never used as a lorry bill

# THE ARTISTS

**Dacres ADAMS** (1864-1951) watercolourist who was educated at Exeter College, Oxford and went on to study with Sir Hubert von Herkomer at Bushey School of Art and then in Munich. He is best known for his very detailed watercolours of architectural subjects, such as 'St John's College, Oxford', and 'Dining Hall, Winchester College'. (28)

**Edgar AINSWORTH** (c.1906-c.1975) painted the friezes at the Imperial Institute in 1929 and designed posters for Shell and the Empire Marketing Board in the 1930s, including 'Buy from the Empire's Gardens'. Best known as a book illustrator, he was art editor of *Picture Post* and after the Second World War went to Belsen to do illustrations for the magazine. In 1948 he wrote an account of the last days of the British in Palestine, illustrated in pen and wash, and his works from Palestine were shown in the exhibition *Six Artists Abroad* organised by the Association of Industrial Artists in 1949. He also exhibited works in pen and wash at the Royal Academy. (60)

**John Stewart ANDERSON** poster artist, studied at Wolverhampton School of Art and the Royal College of Art. (67)

**Edward ARDIZZONE** (1900-1979) painter and illustrator, was born in Haiphong, Indo-China. He worked as a clerk for the Eastern Telegraph Company in London while studying in the evenings at Westminster School of Art. He was most famous for his watercolours of London life. His drawings were published in the *Radio Times* and *Punch,* and he wrote advertising copy for Johnnie Walker whiskey. In 1936 he wrote and illustrated in pen and wash the children's book *Little Tim and the Brave Sea Captain*. He was an official war artist, recording in watercolours the German invasion of France and the North African and Italian campaigns: these were included in his *Diary*

*of a War Artist* (1974). After the war his commissions included brochures for the Ealing Studios. He illustrated nearly 200 books, one of the best known being Walter de la Mare's *Peacock Pie*. He won the Kate Greenaway Medal in 1957 for *Tim All Alone*. Ardizzone taught graphic design at Camberwell School of Art, and later etching and lithography at the Royal College of Art. He was elected RA in 1970 and a Royal Designer for Industry in 1974. (87,108)

**John ARMSTRONG** (1893-1973) painter who studied at St John's Wood Art School after leaving St John's College, Oxford, and began to paint seriously after the First World War. Under the influence of de Chirico, who exhibited in London in 1928, his paintings became surrealist in the 1930s and he joined Unit One in 1933. In the 1930s he designed posters for the GPO, and the 'New Horizon' series for United Steel. He was also an interior designer and designed theatre and ballet sets, and film sets for Alexander Korda, including *The Private Life of Henry VIII* (1933) He also decorated the 'Cave in Harmony' cabaret in Gower Street for Elsa Lanchester. He did large mural paintings, including a series of eight panels for the dining room at Shell-Mex House in 1932, and murals for the ceiling of the Council Chamber at Bristol, the Festival of Britain Centre and the Royal Marsden Hospital. He painted in oil, tempera and gouache, especially small abstract paintings and exhibited regularly at the Royal Academy. He was an official war artist during the Second World War. (48, 56, 94, 103)

**George AYERS** was a poster artist who also designed covers for books and pamphlets. (105)

**John BANTING** (1902-1972) attended Bernard Meninsky's evening classes while working as a bank clerk, and then studied in Paris in

1922 before returning to work for a time as a clerk in his father's book-binding factory. He exhibited with the London Group and with the Surindépendants in Paris during the 1920s and had his first one-man show at the Wertheim Gallery in London in 1929. He also designed ballet sets, including *Pomona* and *Prometheus* at Sadler's Wells in 1929. In 1930 he took a studio in Paris and began to adopt a surrealist style. His work was included in the International Surrealist Exhibition at the new Burlington Galleries in 1936 and in the exhibition *Fantastic Art Dada Surrealism* at the Museum of Modern Art in New York the same year. As art director for Strand Films in 1939 he produced documentaries and became art editor of the magazine *Our Time* in 1941. (20)

**John Roland BARKER** (1911-1959) painter, poster designer and mural painter who studied at the Leicester School of Art and originally wanted to become a portrait painter. After visiting Italy and Paris on a travelling scholarship from the International Guild of Decorators he became a graphic designer in 1934, working as an assistant to Austin Cooper while teaching at Eastbourne School of Art. In the 1930s he designed posters for Shell-Mex, the GPO, the BBC, London Passenger Transport Board, the Orient Line, the Ministry of Labour and HMV, experimenting with the use of photography in posters. In 1950 he won the Poster Design Competition for the British section of the European Recovery Programme. In the 1950s he designed posters, textiles and magazines for Shell, Fisons and ICI. He also painted murals and illustrated books. (9,13)

**Henry Mayo BATEMAN** (1887-1970) Australian cartoonist and illustrator who studied at the Westminster School of Art and then Goldsmiths College School of Art and worked for three years in the London studio of the Dutch painter, Charles van Havenmaet. He began to contribute drawings to the *Tatler* in 1904 and published work in *Punch* from 1915. His cartoons were usually on the theme of social embarrassment, as in *The Man Who* . . . series of cartoons,

for example '*The Man Who Threw a Snowball at St Moritz*', and '*The Guardsman Who Dropped His Rifle*'. He also wrote humorous books, including *Burlesques, Considered Trifles,* and *H.M.Bateman by Himself.* (5)

**Vanessa BELL** (1879-1961) painter and designer, the daughter of Sir Leslie Stephen, first editor of the *Dictionary of National Biography,* and elder sister of Virginia Woolf. She studied at the Royal Academy Schools from 1901 to 1904, where she was influenced by John Singer Sargent, and after the death of her father in 1904 moved to Bloomsbury. In 1907 she married Clive Bell, the art critic, and their home became a focal point of the Bloomsbury circle. Four of her paintings were exhibited in the second Post-Impressionist Exhibition in 1912. She worked with Roger Fry at Omega Workshops from 1913 until their failure in 1919, designing textiles, embroideries, mosaics, painted furniture and also book jackets for the Hogarth Press. From 1913 onwards she lived with the painter and designer Duncan Grant and they worked together decorating houses and furniture. With Duncan Grant she painted the murals at Berwick Church, Sussex from 1940 to 1942. A member of the London Group from 1919, she continued to paint and exhibit still life, landscapes and portraits. Her elder son, the poet Julian Bell, was killed in the Spanish Civil War in 1937. (36)

**Lord BERNERS** (Sir Gerald Hugh Tyrwhitt-Wilson, 5th baronet and 14th baron, 1883-1950) served in the diplomatic service in Constantinople and Rome until he inherited the title in 1918, when he bought Faringdon House in Berkshire and settled there. His chief interest was music, and between 1926 and 1946 he wrote ballet music, beginning with *The Triumph of Neptune* (1926) written for the Diaghilev ballet. He composed three scores for the Sadler's Wells Ballet Company, and for *A Wedding Banquet,* produced in 1937, he designed the costumes as well. He published two volumes of autobiography and five humorous light novels. He was also an art collector and a talented landscape painter in oil, painting in the style of the early Corot, many of whose works he owned. He also painted satirical works in the style of the Douanier Rousseau. (75)

**George BISSILL** (1896-1973) landscape painter and the son of a coal miner who worked in a pit for six years before studying art at Nottingham School of Art from 1920 to 1921. The coal industry is the subject of many of his paintings. He exhibited at the Royal Academy, designed furniture and worked as a pavement artist in London. (42)

**Drake BROOKSHAW**, illustrator and designer who was born in 1907 and taught lithography at Goldsmiths College School of Art. He designed posters for the London Passenger Transport Board and Shell-Mex and did advertisements for ICI, the International Wool Secretariat and Studio Publications. He also did illustrations for the *Radio Times* and for newspapers including the *Daily Mail* and the *Sunday Express.* (58)

**Edwin CALLIGAN** (whose name sometimes appears as Edwin Galligan) taught at Chelsea Polytechnic and designed posters for clients such as Watney's Ales. He also did exhibition work. (54)

**John CASTLE** designed a poster for Hungarian Relief in 1957. (106)

**George CHAPMAN** (1908-1993) painter of the Rhondda Valley who studied at Gravesend School of Art and in the 1930s designed posters for London Transport before enrolling at the Slade School in 1937. He transferred to the Royal College of Art in 1938, studying under Gilbert Spencer. After the Second World War he moved to the artists' colony at Great Bardfield in Essex, while teaching at the London College of Printing. A visit to Wales in 1953 inspired him to start painting the mining communities of the Rhondda Valley, paintings which are often compared to those of L.S. Lowry. By the end of the 1960s his social realism was out of fashion and he stopped painting for ten years. At one point to earn a living he was making mail order collapsible lampshades, but he began to paint again in 1980. (101)

**Verney DANVERS** ran a school of commercial art. In the early1920s he designed posters for the London Underground in the series 'Some Posters of Old Streets' and later produced posters for the LNER (London and North Eastern Railway), including the cover of the *Camping Holidays* booklet in 1934, and for the Southern Region. He had commissions from fashion and interior design companies. (16)

**Robin DARWIN** (1910-1974) painter who was the great-grandson of Charles Darwin. He grew up in Cambridge and studied at the Slade School. From 1933 he had a series of one-man exhibitions, chiefly of watercolours. He was art master at Eton from 1933 to 1938. During the Second World War he served in the Camouflage Directorate, and for a time was based in Leamington Spa, joining the Artists' and Designers' Collective. After the war, while working for the Council of Industrial Design, he produced a report *The Training of the Industrial Designer* proposing radical changes in the curriculum of the Royal College of Art. After two years as Professor of Fine Art at Durham University he was appointed Principal of the Royal College of Art in 1948. He remained Principal until 1967, when the College gained university status, and he became Rector, until his retirement in 1971: this period is known as 'the Darwin era'. He was knighted in 1964 and elected RA in 1972. (100)

**Frank DOBSON** (1886-1963) sculptor who studied painting at Leyton School of Art, Hospitalfield College of Art, Arbroath, Scotland, and City and Guilds School. His first one-man show, at the Chenil Gallery in 1914, was of paintings and drawings. After serving in the Artists' Rifles in the First World War he turned to sculpture, influenced by the work of the French sculptor Maillol, and contributed both sculptures and drawings to the Group X exhibition in 1920. In the 1920s and 1930s he sculpted nude female figures, and became known as a portrait sculptor. He did a bronze head of Osbert Sitwell (1923), and busts of Asquith and Lydia Lopokova and was selected as one of the Six European Sculptors whose work was shown in America in 1924. He was President of the London Group from 1923 to 1927. He was an official war artist during the Second World War and Professor of Sculpture at the Royal College of Art from 1946 to 1953. Among his best works is the figure 'Truth' in the Tate Gallery. He was awarded the CBE in 1947 and elected RA in 1953. (35)

**Pamela DREW** (1910-1989) painter who was born in Burnley, Lancashire, and studied with Dorothy Baker at Christchurch, Hampshire, and with Iain McNab at the Grosvenor School of Modern Art, before studying in Paris with Roger Chastel. She exhibited paintings in oil and pastel of marine and aeroplane subjects. She was the official artist for the RAF Coronation Review in 1953. As an Air Ministry accredited artist she went on a tour of the air force in the Middle East in 1955 and as a war artist went to Port Said and Suez in 1956. (76)

**Jean D'YLEN** (pseudonym of Jean Beguin, 1886-1938) born in Paris, and studied at the Ecole Bernard Palissy, the Ecole d'Application des Beaux-Arts à l'Industrie, and the Ecole des Beaux-Arts. He began as a jewellery designer, but after the First World War concentrated on advertising. He worked for the advertising agency Vercasson from 1920 and had various European clients. He was well known in France in the 1920s, regarded by the journal *La Publicité* as 'the master of the modern poster'. He used imagery related to that of Surrealism: one of his most famous posters was for Spa-Monopole in 1924, with a clown vaulting over a bottle with water fizzing out of the top. From 1928 Wiener and Co. printed his designs in England and he began to design posters for Shell, BP and Esso. From the mid-1930s he published his work independently in France and took part in the Paris International Exhibition in 1937. (6,15)

**Rosemary** (born 1910- ) and **Clifford** (1907-1985) **ELLIS** were married in 1931 and worked together throughout their lives. In the 1930s they designed posters for Shell, the Empire Marketing Board and the GPO, and their posters for London Transport included the famous 'Wolves at Whipsnade' and the 'Summer is Flying' poster on London buses. They designed a mosaic panel for a bathroom for the *British Art in Industry* exhibition at the Royal Academy in 1935 and a mosaic floor for the entrance to the British pavilion at the Paris Exhibition of 1937. They were among a group of artists commissioned by J.Lyons and Co. in 1947 to design lithographs for the Lyons Corner Houses. Between 1943 and 1982 they designed nearly 100 book covers for the *New Naturalist* series published by Collins. Clifford Ellis became head of the Bath School of Art in 1938, which in 1946 moved as the Bath Academy of Art to Corsham Court in Wiltshire, home of Lord Methuen RA. At Corsham Court, a residential art school and teachers' training college, Clifford Ellis, principal until his retirement in 1972, invited leading artists and musicians to teach a wide range of arts and crafts. His pupils included the painter Howard Hodgkin. (61, 62, 63, 84)

**Hans FEIBUSCH** (1898 — ) was born in Frankfurt, the son of a Jewish dentist. He served in the German army on the Russian front from 1916, abandoning his medical studies to study painting at the Berlin Academy, and later in Italy and Paris. In Frankfurt, as a member of the *Frankfurter Künstlerbund,* he began to paint murals. His work was banned by the Nazis and he settled in London in 1933. His paintings were exhibited in the 'Degenerate Art' exhibition in Berlin in 1937. The architect Maxwell Fry commissioned him to do the mural 'Footwashing' in the Methodist Chapel, Colliers Wood, and this led to a series of commissions for church murals from Dr George Bell, Bishop of Chichester. In 1951 he painted the mural 'The Baptism of Christ' in Chichester Cathedral. After the war he did murals for the architect Thomas Ford who was restoring bombed churches. He published *Mural Painting* in 1946. He was a member of the London Group from 1935 and exhibited at the Royal Academy. In the 1970s he turned to sculpture. There was a major retrospective exhibition *Hans Feibusch: the Heat of Vision* in 1995. (52)

**Dominic Charles FOUQUERAY** (1869-1956) studied in Paris. During the First World War he produced many posters, including posters for the Serbian Flag Days, and a dramatic poster of Cardinal Mercier watching over Belgium. He worked as an illustrator, painter and engraver. (7,8)

**Barnett FREEDMAN** (1901-1958) was born in Stepney, the son of Russian Jewish immigrants. For five years he worked as a draughtsman in an architect's office, while studying art at evening classes at St Martin's School of Art. He studied painting at the Royal College of Art and taught still life there, as well as teaching at the Ruskin School of Drawing in Oxford. In the 1930s he designed posters for Shell-Mex, London Transport, the BBC and the GPO, and his work was included in the *British Art In Industry* exhibition at the Royal Academy in 1935. In 1935 his design was selected for the George V Silver Jubilee postage stamp. A pioneer in the revival of colour lithography, he was best known as a book designer and illustrator. In 1930 he illustrated Siegfried Sassoon's *Memoirs of an Infantry Office* for Faber and Faber. From 1941 to 1946 he was an official war artist, first with the army in France, and then with the Royal Navy on the battleship *Repulse* on Arctic convoys to Russia and in submarines. His war paintings include one of the beach at Arromanches on D-Day. He was appointed a Royal Designer for Industry in 1949. (45,46)

**Abram GAMES** (1914-1996) was born in Whitechapel, the son of Latvian Jewish immigrants. He studied at St Martin's School of Art and worked in a commercial art studio until he won first prize in a poster competition to advertise LCC evening classes, when he became a freelance poster designer. In the late 1930s he designed posters for Shell, London Transport, the GPO and the Co-operative Building Society. From 1941 to 1946 he was an official poster designer for the Public Relations department of the War Office, designing such famous posters as 'Your Talk May Kill Your Comrades' and 'When you Go Out, Don't Crow about – the Things you know about'. He lectured on graphic design at the Royal College of Art and continued to design posters: it was he who did the 'Top People Take *The Times*' series for *The Times*. He also designed symbols, including those for the Festival of Britain and the Queen's Award for Industry. He was awarded the OBE in 1958, and was appointed a Royal Designer for Industry in 1959. *Over My Shoulder* was published in 1960. He was also an inventor whose patents included the 1959 Cona coffee portable model. (97)

**Tom GENTLEMAN** (1892-1966) was born in Coatbridge, Lanarkshire and was apprenticed to the family drapery firm. He studied art at evening classes at Glasgow School of Art and eventually became a full-time painting student there. After service in the Glasgow Yeomanry and Scottish Rifles during the First World War he went to Europe on a travelling scholarship. He spent several years working as a cartoonist and illustrator on Glasgow papers before moving to London in 1928 to work for Crawford's advertising agency, with Edward McKnight Kauffer and Ashley Havindon. In the 1930s he moved around various agencies, designing posters for clients such as London Transport. He then became head of the Shell Studio at Shell-Mex under Jack Beddington. During the Second World War he worked in the Ministry of Information and then returned to the Shell Studio, although he no longer ran it. He retired in 1952. He painted a large mural of an English garden at teatime on a summer's day, with scenes of his family at home in Hertford, for the Kardomah Café in the rue de Rivoli, Paris. He also wrote and illustrated a children's book *Brae Farm*, about his childhood experiences on the Clyde. His print, 'White Horses' (1945) is well known. (79, 81)

**Eric GEORGE** (1881-1961) was an undergraduate at Oriel College, Oxford, and went on to study at the Westminster School of Art and the Académie Julian in Paris. He was known mainly as a painter of portraits and figure designs in oil and he exhibited at the Royal Academy, the Modern Society of Portrait Painters and the New English Art Club. He published a book on the painter Benjamin Robert Haydon in 1947. (43)

**Duncan GRANT** (1885-1978) was born in Scotland but spent his early childhood in India. He studied at the Westminster School of Art while living with his cousins, the Stracheys, and then in Paris and at the Slade School. He was one of the first English artists to be influenced by the Fauves and by Cézanne, and he exhibited at the second Post-Impressionist Exhibition in 1912. He was part of the Bloomsbury circle and from 1913 lived with the painter Vanessa Bell. In 1913 he joined Roger Fry as a director of the Omega Workshops.

While continuing to paint and exhibit regularly with the London Group, he worked on various decorative projects, many with Vanessa Bell, including designs for textiles, pottery, stage sets and costumes. They were commissioned to do the decorations for the new Cunard liner the *Queen Mary* in 1935 but their murals were rejected. In 1940-42 they decorated the church at Berwick in Sussex. Duncan Grant was appointed a Royal Designer for Industry in 1941 for his work on printed textiles. (50)

**Richard GUYATT** (1914 – ) designed posters for Shell-Mex and BP in 1935. During the Second World War he was Regional Camouflage Officer for Scotland for the Ministry of Home Security. He was director and chief designer for Cockade from 1946 to 1948 and was one of the designers from the Royal College of Art for the Lion and Unicorn Pavilion at the Festival of Britain in 1951. He was responsible for a display representing the British Law. From the 1950s he was a consultant designer for companies such as Josiah Wedgwod and Sons, the British Sugar Bureau and W H Smith. He did ceramic designs for several British embassies, King's College Cambridge, the Goldsmiths' Company, and designed commemorative mugs for the Coronation in 1953, the Investiture of Prince Charles in 1969, and the Royal Silver Wedding in 1972. He also designed stamps, including a stamp celebrating the 700th anniversary of parliament in 1965 and the 1977 Silver Jubilee stamps. He designed a commemorative crown piece for the Queen Mother's 80th birthday. Richard Guyatt was Professor of Graphic Art at the Royal College of Art from 1948 to 1978 and Rector 1978-81. (73,95)

**Frederick Clifford HARRISON** was born in 1901 and studied at Hammersmith College of Art and the Central School of Arts and Crafts. He worked for Publicity Arts Ltd in the 1920s. (27)

**Tristram HILLIER** (1905-1983) painter who was born in Peking, and later went back there to learn Chinese. He studied under Henry Tonks at the Slade School, and then in Paris at the Atelier Colarossi, where he met many of the Surrealist painters. Influenced by Max Ernst and de Chirico, he was part of the British surrealist *avant-garde* in the 1930s, and a member of the Unit One group in 1934, while travelling in France and Spain. He lived and worked in France from 1937 until the German invasion in 1940. After the war he settled in Somerset. He was elected RA in 1967. (65,77)

**James HOLLAND** (1905-1996), trained at Rochester School of Art and the Royal College of Art as a painter but decided that graphic art was a more significant form of communication in the world of the 1930s: 'I want to show the chaotic life under an inadequate and decaying social structure'. A member of the Communist Party, he was one of the founders of the Artists International Association in 1933 and exhibited *The Social Scene* in the AIA exhibition in 1934. He exhibited in Moscow in 1935 and in 1937 was one of the members of the AIA at the Paris World Fair, decorating rooms for the Peace Pavilion. In his satirical political cartoons and drawings for the *Left Review* he often used textual quotations, as in 'With a ladder . . .' (1934). He worked for the Ministry of Information as a poster and exhibition designer, and was appointed Chief Exhibitions Designer of the Festival of Britain in 1948. In the 1950s he pursued a successful career in advertising design. He was President of the Society of Industrial Artists 1960-61 and Education Officer 1971-79. In 1980 he published *Minerva at Fifty*, the history of the Society. (31)

**Harold HUSSEY** worked in the post-war Shell Studio at Shell-Mex House. (98)

**Foster JARRETT** designed a series of posters for the National Employment Exchange Service in the 1930s. (34)

**Andrew JOHNSON** studied at the Central School of Arts and Crafts. He worked for various advertising agencies, designing posters for LNER (London and North Eastern Railways) in the 1920s and 1930s, including 'Fort William' and 'Woodhall Spa'. In the 1920s he did posters for Lever Brothers, Lux and *The Times*. In the 1930s he designed posters for General Motors and Moss Bros, and brochures for the Legal and General Assurance Company. (32)

**Mary KESSELL** (1914-1977) designer, book illustrator, mural decorator and painter who studied at Clapham School of Arts and Crafts 1935-37 and at the Central School of Arts and Crafts 1937-39. While still a student she illustrated T. Moult's *Best Poems of 1937*. As an official war artist she worked in Germany in 1945. She had her first one-man show in 1950 at the Leicester Galleries. She worked for the post-war Shell Studio at Shell-Mex House and designed murals for Westminster Hospital and for Imperial Chemical House, Millbank. Mary Kessell lectured in drawing at the London School of Painting from 1957. She was married to the poster designer Tom Eckersley. (104)

**Jock KINNEIR** (1917-1994) graphic designer and exhibition and display designer who produced a poster for Shell while still a student. He worked for the Central Office of Information from 1946 to 1949 and then for the Design Research Unit. His work there included a stand for Monsanto Chemicals at the British Industries Fair in 1950, and the design for the exhibition of Irish industrial design in 1956. He arranged displays for the Foreign Office and the Admiralty, did work for P&O and Decca Records, and published cartoons in *Night and Day* and engravings in *Signature*. He is best known for his designs for Britain's signing systems of roads, airports, the army, railways and hospitals. He was Head of Graphic Design at the Royal College of Art from 1964 to 1969. (72)

**David LEWIS** designed posters for London Transport in the 1950s in the series 'Enjoy your London'. (66)

**Edward McKNIGHT KAUFFER** (1891-1954) the American poster designer was born in Great Falls, Montana, and studied in San Francisco and Chicago before going to Paris to the Académie Moderne 1913-14. In 1914 he settled in England. A founder member of the Vorticist Group X, he gave up painting after the failure of Group X in 1920. He designed his first poster for London Underground Railways in 1915 and this led to many commissions from Frank Pick of London Underground between 1915 and 1940. Among his best known posters is 'Soaring to Success! Daily Herald – The Early Bird' (1919). His posters in the 1920s, with their geometric designs, were strongly influenced by Cubism and Vorticism. In 1924 he published *The Art of the Poster*. He was a close friend of T.S.Eliot, and illustrated his *Ariel Poems* (1927-31) for Faber and Faber and designed the sets for the ballet *Checkmate* for Ninette de Valois at Sadler's Wells in 1937. He was appointed an honorary Royal Designer for Industry in 1937. He returned to America in 1941. Edward McKnight Kauffer is regarded by some as the greatest poster designer of the 20th century, a figure comparable to Toulouse-Lautrec in the history of poster design. (37, 38, 40, 41, 71, 80, 96)

**Cathleen MANN** (1896-1959) painter of landscapes, flowers and portraits and the daughter of the Scottish portrait painter, Harrington Mann. She studied at the Slade School and in Paris. She subsequently exhibited regularly at the Royal Academy and the Royal Society of Portrait Painters, with several one-man exhibitions at London galleries. During the Second World War she was an official war artist, employed mainly as a portrait painter. After the war she was influenced by the painter Matthew Smith (her portrait of him is in the National Portrait Gallery). Her best work was done in the last ten years of her life. (53, 90)

**MARC** This may be Marc (Mark) Severin, who was born in 1906 in Brussels, studied at Ghent University and lived in England during the First World War. His work appeared regularly in German magazines from 1927 and he designed posters. He moved to England in 1932 and worked as an advertising designer and book illustrator, and designed posters for the Southern Railways. He became art director of the advertising agency, R.C.Casson. During the Second World War he was in Belgium but came back to England from 1945 to 1949, working for ICI and OUP, before returning to

Belgium as Professor of Engraving at the Institut Supérieur des Beaux Arts in Antwerp, a post he held until 1972. Another possible 'Marc' is Marc Stone, who designed war posters, including 'Libya – Help them finish the job'. (22)

**Maurice MILES** had a studio in St John's Wood. He exhibited a painting of a studio interior at the Royal Academy in 1931 and designed two posters for the London Underground in the 1930s, one for Kew Gardens and the other for the Zoo, which was exhibited in the *British Art in Industry* exhibition at the Royal Academy in 1935. (59)

**Jack MILLER** painter, was born c.1920. Jack Beddington gave him his first commission, 'Summer Shell Mermaids', at the age of sixteen while he was still a student at Goldsmiths' School of Art. He had a studio in Chelsea. (69)

**Robert MILLER** was an advertising illustrator. He was a member of the Society of Industrial Artists and Designers. (74)

**Sir Cedric MORRIS** (9th baronet, 1889-1982). Born in Wales, he was one of the finest 20th century British painters of flowers and garden produce as well as birds, animals, landscapes, and portraits. He worked for a time as a farmer in Canada but returned to Wales and then enrolled at the Académie Delacluse in Paris in 1914. He joined the Artists' Rifles in 1914 but was later discharged. In 1918 he met the painter Arthur Lett-Haines, with whom he lived for sixty years. In 1920 he moved to Paris and studied at the Académie Moderne. His first one-man show, in Rome in 1922, was closed by the Fascists. Back in England in 1926, he was elected to the Seven and Five Society. He and Arthur Lett-Haines moved to Suffolk in 1935 and in 1937 founded the East Anglian School of Painting and Drawing: their students included Lucien Freud and Maggi Hambling. He lectured in design at the Royal College of Art from 1950 to 1953. His paintings are internationally known, and include

*Herstmonceux Church, Mill in Brittany* and *Farmyard, Dorset.* Throughout his life he collected rare species of plants and was known as a breeder of irises. (64)

**Charles MOZLEY** (1914-1991) went to the Sheffield School of Art at the age of eleven and then won a scholarship to the Royal College of Art in 1933. He taught at the Camberwell School of Art 1938-39. During the Second World War he was a Lieutenant-Colonel in military intelligence, involved in work on camouflage. After the war he worked mainly on book illustrations and book jackets for English and American publishers until he became known for his murals for the Festival of Britain in 1951. In the 1950s he designed a number of film posters for Ealing Studios, including *The Second Mrs Tanqueray* (1954), and posters for BEA and the Midland Bank. In 1957 he designed the 'Mind That Child' poster. (89, 92, 93)

**Paul NASH** (1889-1946) studied at Chelsea Polytechnic and at the Slade School. He joined the Artists' Rifles in 1914, but after he was wounded at Ypres in 1917 he was sent back to the front as an official war artist. In his most famous war painting, *The Menin Road*, he created strange patterns out of the devastated landscape of the Western front. A member of the New English Art Club and the London Group, he painted a series of watercolours of Dymchurch beach in Kent in the 1920s. In the 1930s he was one of a group of *avant-garde* artists influenced by Surrealism and he founded the group Unit One in 1933, exhibiting at the International Surrealist Exhibitions of 1936 and 1938. In the 1930s he designed textiles, ceramics, theatre sets, posters, book jackets and wrote the *Shell Guide to Dorset.* He became fascinated by prehistoric burial mounds and stones in fields and this influenced his landscape painting. He also became interested in photography and took thousands of photographs, many of which he used as studies for his paintings. He was an official war artist to the Air Ministry, and later to the Ministry of Information. (51, 68, 85)

**Ben NICHOLSON** (1894-1982) abstract artist who was the son of the painter Sir William Nicholson. He studied at the Slade School before travelling to France and Italy. Between 1925 and 1936 he exhibited with the Seven and Five Society, and in the 1930s he became a leading *avant-garde* artist. In 1933 he was a founder member of Unit One and with the sculptor Barbara Hepworth (who later became his second wife) he joined the Paris group, Abstraction-Création, in 1933. Influenced by the work of Mondrian he developed his style of geometrical reliefs, and created his first all-white reliefs in 1934 – his major contribution to Modernism. His work was shown in the exhibition *Cubism and Abstract Art* at the Museum of Modern Art in New York in 1936. He co-edited *Circle,* a survey of constructivist art, in 1937. In 1939 he moved to St Ives, in Cornwall, and became the centre of an artists' colony. There he continued to paint abstract works, but also more naturalistic paintings and drawings. He did a mural for the Festival of Britain in 1951. He moved to Switzerland in 1958 and concentrated on carved reliefs. He was awarded the OM in 1968. (88)

**Charles PAINE** studied at Salford College of Art and the Royal College of Art and later taught at Edinburgh College of Art. He designed nineteen posters and three panel posters for London Underground between 1920 and 1929, including 'Hampton Court by Train', and the famous Zoo poster 'Penguins', which was reproduced in magazines all over the world as an example of British poster art. While working for the Baynard Press he did posters and advertisements for a wide range of companies. (25)

**John PIPER** (1903-1992) worked as an articled clerk in his father's solicitor's office before studying at Richmond School of Art and the Royal College of Art. He turned to abstract art in the 1930s. He became a member of the Seven and Five Society in 1934 and edited the *avant-garde* quarterly *Axis* in 1935 but rejected abstraction in 1937, and began to paint romantic views of landscapes and great houses in decay. He collaborated with his friend John Betjeman on the *Shell Guides* to the counties of England. As an official war artist he recorded the devastation of Coventry Cathedral in November 1940. After the war he designed a number of stage sets for Benjamin Britten, beginning with *The Rape of Lucretia* at Glyndebourne in 1946. With Osbert Lancaster he helped to design the Battersea Pleasure Gardens for the Festival of Britain in 1951 and in the late 1950s he began to work in stained glass, and did a stained glass wall for the Baptistry in Coventry Cathedral. He also did a window for Liverpool Cathedral and designed the Britten Memorial Window in Aldeburgh parish church. John Piper was made a Companion of Honour in 1972. (107)

**Tom PURVIS** (1888-1959) trained at the Camberwell School of Art before studying with Sickert and Dégas. After six years working for an advertising agency he became a freelance designer, starting with a poster for Dewar's whiskey in 1907. He served with the Artists' Rifles in France, and then became a war artist for the Ministry of Supply. His poster style, with its use of flat, massed colours, was influenced by that of the Beggarstaff Brothers. Among his best known posters are those for the LNER, including the two sets 'East Coast Joys' and 'East Coast Resorts' (1925), each of which form one continuous coastline when joined together, and the 'Coronation' crossing the Royal Border Bridge, Berwick-upon-Tweed, in the 'It's Quicker by Rail' series (1938). He did a lot of work for Austin Reed and the Canadian Pacific Railways, and also designed a series of posters for the British Industries Fair 1932-34. He was vice-president of the Royal Society of Arts and was appointed a Royal Designer for Industry in 1936. In 1940 he published *Poster Progress*. He was an official war artist for the Ministry of Supply. Late in life he turned to religious painting. (12,17, 23, 26, 33)

**John REYNOLDS** (1909-1935). Son of the art editor of *Punch,* he was a book illustrator and cartoonist, best known for his illustrations for *1066 and All That* (1930). It was he who changed the poster logo of Shell from 'That's Shell That Is!' to 'That's Shell That Was!'. He committed suicide at the age of twenty-six. (57)

**Leonard ROSOMAN** (1913- ) studied at the King Edward VII School of Art at Durham University, the Royal Academy Schools, and the Central School of Arts and Crafts. He was an official war artist to the Admiralty from 1943 to 1945 – an exhibition of his war paintings was held at the Imperial War Museum in 1959 – and he later taught illustration at the Camberwell School of Art and mural decoration at Edinburgh College of Art. He taught at the Royal College of Art from 1957 to 1978. Best known for his paintings of people in interiors, he also painted murals, including murals for the Festival of Britain in 1951, the British Pavilion at the Brussels World Fair in 1958, Harewood House in 1959 and Lambeth Palace Chapel in 1988. He was elected RA in 1969 and was awarded the OBE in 1981. (78)

**Hooper ROWE** designed a number of posters for Shell and BP in the 1930s. (39)

**Hans SCHLEGER** (1898-1976) one of the most influential graphic artists of the twentieth century. He came from a German Jewish family and studied in Berlin and was influenced by the Bauhaus teaching and by poster artists such as A.M.Cassandre. He spent five years working for advertising agencies in New York and adopted the signature 'Zéro'. He settled in London in 1932 and in the 1930s designed posters for Shell-Mex and BP, London Transport and the GPO. He also designed the London bus stop in 1935, and the Highway Code exhibition for the Ministry of Labour in 1938. During the Second World war he did posters for the Ministry of Agriculture, including posters in the 'Grow your Own' and 'Dig for Victory' series. After the war he was one of the originators of the idea of the 'corporate image' for large businesses and organisations, providing corporate identities for Mac Fisheries (1952-59) and the British Sugar Corporation (1961-75). He also designed logos for the Design Centre in the Haymarket (1955), the Edinburgh International Festival (1966), Hutchinson publishers, John Lewis and Penguin Books. Hans Schleger was appointed a Royal Designer for Industry in 1959. (91)

**Edward SCROGGIE** figure and portrait painter who was born in 1906 and studied at Eastbourne School of Art. He later exhibited at the Royal Society of British Artists and was a member of the Artists International Association in the 1930s. (82)

**Charles SHAW** This may be Charles Shaw (1892-1974), the American abstract painter, who travelled widely in Europe in the 1920s exhibiting his work. He was strongly influenced by Cubism. He also wrote novels and poems and contributed to magazines such as *Vanity Fair* and the *New Yorker*. (70)

**A. STUART-HILL** (died 1948) had a studio in Chelsea and was known as a portrait and landscape painter. He exhibited regularly at the Royal Academy between 1920 and 1947. His London scenes of the Thames from different viewpoints, painted in the 1930s, and his portraits, very often of mayors, were exhibited at the Royal Society of Portrait Painters. (49)

**Rowland SUDDABY** (1912-1973) landscape painter in watercolour and oil who was born in Yorkshire and trained at the Sheffield College of Art and the Royal College of Art. His first job was working for a Wardour Street film studio, ornamenting the titles of black and white films. A member of the Seven and Five Society, he had the first of several one-man exhibitions at the Redfern Gallery in 1934, and later at the Leger Gallery. He moved to Suffolk in 1939 and helped to save Thomas Gainsborough's house in Sudbury. He established a living arts centre there where he was curator for the last four years of his life. (83)

**Graham SUTHERLAND** (1903-1980) began as an engineering apprentice, before studying at Goldsmiths' School of Art. He worked as a printmaker but then became a commercial artist. His earliest commissioned work was for Jack Beddington at Shell and he went on to design many posters for London Transport, as well as glass, china and textiles. He also took up painting, exhibiting in the International Surrealist Exhibition in 1936. He was an official war artist, painting scenes of bomb devastation, and also Cornish tin mines, blast furnaces, iron foundries and limestone quarries. He painted a large Crucifixion for the church of St Matthew, Northampton, and *The Origins of the Land* for the Festival of Britain. He spent much of his time after the war in the south of France. One of his most famous works is the vast *Christ in Glory* tapestry commissioned in 1952 for Coventry Cathedral. He painted his first portrait, an expressionist portrait of Somerset Maugham, in 1949. This led to the commission from the Houses of Parliament to paint Sir Winston Churchill in 1954. The painting was secretly destroyed soon afterwards on the orders of Lady Churchill. He was awarded the OM in 1960. (44, 47, 86)

**VIC** may have been the French poster artist who worked for the advertising agency Etablissements Vercasson at the end of the 1920s and beginning of the 1930s, and signed himself 'Vic'. (24, 30)

**René VINCENT** (1879-1936) trained as an architect at the Ecole des Beaux-Arts in Paris, but then worked for magazines such as *La Vie Parisienne, L'Illustration* and *Fémina,* and for satirical journals, before pursuing a career in advertising in the 1920s. One of his favourite subjects was the automobile (perhaps because he was one of the first people to hold a driving licence), and he designed famous posters for companies such as Bugatti, Citroën and Peugeot. He was also known for his fashion posters, and a series in 1928 advertising winter sports. He later turned to interior decoration, designing dinner services, lamps and vases in the Art Déco style. He sometimes worked under the name René Mael. (14)

**Joseph WEBB** (1908-1962) engraver, studied at Hospitalfields Art College, Arbroath, Scotland. He was known for his etchings of architectural subjects and landscapes and exhibited widely, regularly exhibiting his etchings at the Royal Academy between 1929 and 1947. He also worked as a portrait painter and painted murals. In the 1930s he taught at Chiswick Art School and in the 1940s at the Hammersmith School of Art. He was elected RE (Royal Society of Painter-Etchers and Engravers) in 1930. (99)

**Rex WHISTLER** (1905-1944) mural painter, book illustrator and stage designer who studied at the Slade School from 1922 to 1926 and then in Rome. His most famous work is his mural *The Pursuit of Rare Meats,* commissioned for the new refreshment room at the Tate Gallery, opened in 1927. The success of this led to other mural commissions, including one for the Park Lane house of Lady Louis Mountbatten. He illustrated the Cresset Press edition of *Gulliver's Travels* in 1930, and designed book covers for B.T. Batsford Ltd. He also designed scenery and costumes for operas and plays, including *The Rake's Progress* at Sadler's Wells in 1935. His London Underground poster, 'Britannia visits the British Museum', is full of exuberant baroque detail, and typical of his witty style. He was commissioned in the Welsh Guards in 1939 and was killed in action in Normandy in 1944. He was the brother of the glass engraver Laurence Whistler. (55)

**YUNGE**. Nothing is known of this artist. (29)

## Acknowledgements

Shell UK Limited would like to thank the following people and organisations
for their help in researching the biographies of the artists:
Anne Baker, Research Associate, *New Dictionary of National Biography*
Heather Butler, Manager of the Shell Art Collection
Ivone Martins, Archives Assistant, BP Archive, University of Warwick
Susan Bennett, Archivist, Royal Society of Arts
National Art Library, Victoria and Albert Museum
John Hewitt, Manchester Metropolitan University

If anyone has any further information about the artists featured in this book,
Shell UK would be grateful if you could please forward your comments to:

The Manager of the Shell Art Collection
The National Motor Museum
Beaulieu
Brockenhurst
Hampshire
SO42 7ZN